DATE DUE

MAR 1 3 2000			

GAYLORD | | | PRINTED IN U.S.A.

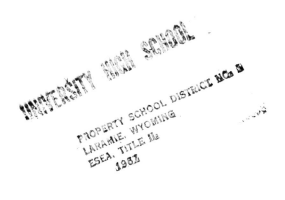

CASTLES

CASTLES

By Fon W. Boardman, Jr.

New York   Henry Z. Walck, Inc.   1957

ACKNOWLEDGMENTS

MANY PERSONS *and organizations were most friendly and helpful to me in the task of securing the photographs and other illustrations needed for this book. I only regret I could not use all the pictures; nor can I here give credit to all the individuals who deserve it. For the record, the photographs on the pages indicated came from the following sources:*

Aerophotos, Dublin, Ireland, 49; Arab Information Center, New York, 36; Austrian Information Service, New York, 66, 67; Belgian Government Information Center, New York, 71, 72; British Information Services, New York, 12, 17, 41, 42, 43, 46, 47, 48, 90, 91, 93, 96; Danish National Travel Service, New York, 73; French Embassy Press and Information Division, New York, 39, 52, 53, 54, 56 (top); French Government Tourist Office, New York, 56 (bottom); German Tourist Information Office, New York, 63, 65; Italian State Tourist Office, New York, 61, 62; Spanish Tourist Office, New York, 58, 59; Consulate General of Switzerland, New York, 69, 70; Mrs. Elisabeth M. Vaudrin, New York, 68.

The illustrations on pages 24, 55, 76, 79-84, and 86 were specially drawn for the book by Frederick T. Chapman.

The plans of five British castles on pages 15, 44, 92, and 94 are reproduced from pamphlets issued by the Ministry of Works and with the permission of the Controller of Her Britannic Majesty's Stationery Office.

F. W. B., Jr.

CONTENTS

GLOSSARY

Bailey The area inside the walls of a motte-and-bailey castle. See *ward*.

Balista A siege weapon, like an enormous crossbow, for firing arrows or stones.

Barbican A small fort outside the gate, used as a first defense of the gate itself.

Battering ram A large beam used to try to knock down a wall.

Battlement An indented *parapet* at the top of a wall.

Belfry A wooden tower, built by the besiegers of a castle and intended to be moved up against the walls of the castle.

Bore Like a battering ram, but smaller and lighter. Used to make a hole in bottom of wall as a starting point for further undermining.

Castle In the Middle Ages, a fortified dwelling place of a noble or a king.

Catapult A giant slingshot that could throw stones or other missiles against a castle.

Corbel A projection from a wall to support the weight of battlement construction.

Courtyard Same as *ward* and *bailey*.

Crenel Same as *embrasure*.

Crenellated Having *battlements*.

Curtain Same as *wall*.

Donjon A great tower, or *keep*. (French).

Drawbridge. A bridge over a moat, part of which could be raised from the castle side by chains or ropes.

Dungeon A deep, dark cell—but comes originally from *donjon* which means tower rather than prison cell.

Embrasure An opening in a parapet wall.

Escalade   To try to climb up and get over a castle wall by means of ladders.

Gatehouse   The strongly defended entrance, often with living quarters, of a castle.

Hall, or *Great Hall*   The principal building within a concentric castle. Like a medieval house set down inside a castle.

Keep   A great tower, or *donjon*, of a castle. Used later to apply to "rectangular" and "shell" keeps.

Machicolations   Openings between *corbels* of a *parapet*.

Merlons   The parts of *parapet* walls between *embrasures*.

Moat   A ditch around a castle, filled with water.

Motte   A mound of earth on which the *keep* of early castles was built.

Parapet   A low wall or barrier at the edge of the top of a wall or tower.

Penthouse   A shelter, of a lean-to type, built to protect men mining or carrying on other operations against a castle, such as using a battering ram.

Portcullis   A wooden gate, shod with iron and suspended by chains, that could be raised and lowered as required.

Postern   A small gate; a "back door" to a castle.

Trebuchet   A gigantic see-saw that could throw very heavy missiles at a castle.

Wall   The high structure around a castle courtyard. The main defense of a castle. The *curtain* of a castle.

Ward   The area inside the walls of a castle. Same as *bailey* and *courtyard*.

CASTLES

I   The Story of a Famous Castle

IN 1468, NEARLY 500 years ago, one of the strongest and most famous castles in the world was captured. The name of this castle was Harlech.

Harlech had been besieged before, but this particular attack was one of the last battles of the savage Wars of the Roses, which were struggles between two noble English families for the throne. One of these was the House of Lancaster and its emblem was the red rose; the other was the House of York and its emblem was the white rose. Soldiers of the Yorkists besieged the castle, which by then was the last one in all of England and Wales held by the forces of Lancaster.

Many Welshmen took part, and the siege inspired a song which is still well known. It is the battle song of the Welsh and is called "Men of Harlech." The melody is often used today as a high school or college song with different words, of course, but the Welsh in those days sang, in their own language:

> "Men of Harlech, in the hollow,
> Do ye hear, like rushing billow
> Wave on wave that surging follow
>   Battle's distant sound?
> 'Tis the tramp of Saxon foemen,
> Saxon spearmen, Saxon bowmen,
> Be they knights or hinds or yeomen,
>   They shall bite the ground!"

Harlech Castle had been attacked, off and on, for more than seven

Harlech Castle,

Wales

years. When it finally surrendered in 1468, there were about 50 able-bodied persons left in it. One of these was a twelve-year-old boy who was destined to become King Henry VII of England.

Harlech Castle stood, and still stands, on the west coast of north Wales, which is now part of Great Britain. Even in 1468 Harlech was nearly 200 years old. The building of castles in England had begun another 200 years before that, and even earlier in other parts of Europe. Thus it is now about 1,000 years since men began building castles.

This structure is an example of castle building in its greatest period. When Harlech was begun in 1285, men had had several hundred years experience in building, defending, and besieging castles. Like many other castles in Britain and in other countries, Harlech was placed on the most easily defended site, and was designed to withstand the best weapons the attackers had in those days before the use of gunpowder in cannons.

Harlech Castle was built on a rocky summit, about 200 feet high. This in itself made it difficult and discouraging for anyone to attack.

On two sides, the west and the north, were steep, rocky cliffs, at the foot of which were marshes and the sea, although the water does not now come as near the castle as it did then. A deep ditch, filled with water, was dug around the other two sides. This ditch, or moat, was from 30 to 60 feet wide. Because of its site, Harlech was constructed almost square. The great castles of this period were more or less square or rectangular, but all were shaped so as best to fit the land on which they were built.

The main part of the castle—within the high walls and towers—occupied less than half the total area. The steep, rocky ground on the west and north was an open space, without buildings, and was called the outer ward, or outer bailey. It was not even entirely surrounded by walls and some of the fortifications in this area were not built until long after the main part of the castle. There was a water gate so that supplies could be brought by sea as well as by land.

Outside the main wall of the castle and about 30 feet from it was another wall only a few yards high, known as the outer wall, or outer curtain. It was the first line of defense on the south and east and was built low so that the soldiers on the main walls and on the high towers could fire their weapons over the heads of the defenders on this outer wall.

The main defense of the castle, the inner wall or inner curtain, was very high with great round towers jutting out at each corner. All of this was made of large stones, or masonry work. The main entrance was on the eastern side of the castle and everything about it was planned to make it impossible for attackers to get into the castle through the gate. First of all, on the far side of the moat was a small stone fort known as a barbican, although the one at Harlech no longer stands. Beyond this was a bridge over the moat, partly of stone, with a drawbridge that could be raised from the castle side of the moat.

Just on the castle side, an outer gate was built, it too being a small fort in itself. Beyond this, and forming part of the main wall of the castle, was the gatehouse, the dominant feature of the whole castle.

13

It was three stories high and was designed as the residence of the constable, or commander, of the castle, with living rooms on the upper floors and storerooms in the basement. In fact, if there should be treachery in the garrison of a castle as there sometimes was, the commander and those faithful to him could use the gatehouse as a fortress against those holding the rest of the castle. The gatehouse was two elongated twin towers with a roofed-over passageway between. This gatehouse had a portcullis at either end. A portcullis was a large gate, made of a wooden frame covered with iron sheets, with spikes at the bottom. It was suspended by chains so that it could be raised and lowered—and dropped on the heads of attackers if they got caught under it. Both the walls of the gatehouse and the roof over the passageway had slits so that any foe who got inside the portcullis could be fired upon from all directions.

The roofs of the gatehouse and the corner towers were almost flat and were covered with lead. The tops of the walls, both the low outer ones and the high inner ones, were embattled, which means that they had gaps in them at the top through which the defenders could fire and then duck behind the adjoining higher piece of wall. The effect was something like a row of giant teeth, with every other tooth missing.

The area inside the main walls of such a castle as Harlech was called the inner ward. In most castles it was not as big as usually imagined. At Harlech it was about 160 by 130 feet, not as long either way as a football field. In the inner ward, and built against the sides of the walls, were the domestic buildings used by the people who lived in the castle. At Harlech the bakehouse and the chapel were built against the northern curtain. The chapel had a lean-to roof with an arched wood and plaster ceiling. Here too, and partly built into the wall, was the well which supplied the garrison with water. Against the west wall were the great hall, the buttery and pantry, and the kitchens. The great hall was like an ordinary house of the period, set down inside a castle. It was the center of domestic life where the people had their meals and spent their leisure time. It was 60 by 27

14

1286-90 (ORIGINAL PLAN)

1286-90 (MODIFICATION DURING BUILDING)

LATER MEDIAEVAL

feet. The granary was on the south wall, with a large cellar beneath because a castle had to be able to store enough food to feed the garrison for many months. Otherwise the garrison in the castle might have to surrender even though the attackers had not been able to get inside the castle.

Harlech Castle had a second gate, on the north, called the postern. This was not as elaborately constructed as the main gate, but was placed where it was difficult to get at it at all. Such gates were sometimes used by a garrison to escape if a castle was about to be captured. They were also used to let messengers, spies, and scouts in and out.

This is a brief description of Harlech Castle. It took a great deal of time and money, and men and materials, to build it. The English kings thought it was worth it because for many years, especially after the Normans conquered England in the eleventh century, these English kings had been trying to control the area known as Wales, and the inhabitants, the Welsh people. They won and lost many battles, but they never succeeded until the thirteenth century when Edward I was king. Edward had tried and failed in 1257, before he was king.

Plan of Harlech Castle, Wales

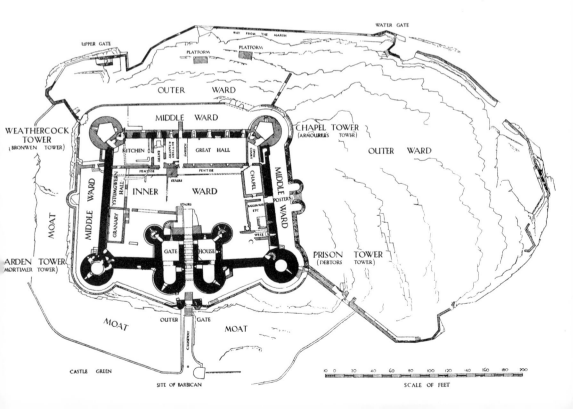

He was only 18 years old then, but he was already a skillful commander of troops. He became king in 1272, and between 1277 and 1282 he finally succeeded in conquering Wales, although the Welsh revolted many times after that.

Even though Edward I crushed Welsh resistance and proclaimed Wales to be part of the English king's dominions, he knew he would have to use force to keep the Welsh subdued. The best way to do this in those days was to build large, strong castles which rebellious nobles and their followers could not capture. The castles also served as central strong points which could house well-trained troops who could use the castles as their headquarters and could go out from them to put down any uprising.

Therefore, Edward started to build the most imposing and powerful castles the British Isles had ever seen. There were eight of them in north Wales: Builth, Flint, Rhuddlan, Conway, Caernarvon, Beaumaris, Aberystwyth, and Harlech. In most cases, although not at Harlech, a whole town was included within the plan of fortification. Edward's son, who was to become King Edward II, was born in Caernarvon Castle and in 1301 he was proclaimed Prince of Wales, a title it has been customary ever since to confer on the male heir to the British throne.

It took skill and experience to supervise the building of these massive structures, and Edward employed experts for the work, particularly one man known as Master James of St. George. In accounts of the cost of building these castles he is called "the master of the King's works in Wales." Probably Edward met him in Savoy, where Master James had acquired his skill and experience. He was a man of both technical and administrative ability. As salary he received three shillings a day which was a large sum at that time.

The old records show that to build castles, such as Harlech, it was necessary to bring from far and near masons, carpenters, quarrymen, diggers, smiths, and carters. Dwellings and workshops had to be erected for the men, and there might be as many as 400 masons working at once to build the walls and towers. In all more than 1,000 men would work for three or four years to build a castle like Harlech, and hundreds of shiploads or cartloads of materials would have to be brought to the scene. Work on Harlech began about 1285 when the ditch in front of the castle was cut in the rocks, but it was not finished until about 1290. By that time more than £8,000 had been spent. In all, King Edward spent about £80,000 on his castle building in Wales, a very great sum in those days. Today it would probably cost at least $2,000,000 to build such a castle as Harlech.

Caernarvon Castle, Wales

Even these powerful castles did not keep the Welsh from revolting against English rule. While Edward I was still king and after he had built Harlech and other castles, several of them were besieged. In 1295 Harlech was besieged by the Welsh under Madoc ap Llewelyn. Although the garrison numbered only 37 men they held out until they were relieved. It was necessary to bring help by sea because the attackers had cut off the castle by land.

Harlech Castle was involved in the last and most serious of the Welsh uprisings against the English, which came more than 100 years after Edward I thought he had conquered the country. The Welsh hero who led this fight, and whose name above all others is associated with Harlech, was Owen Glendower, who was born in 1354. In 1400, angered by a personal grievance against an English lord for which he could get no satisfaction, Glendower began to attack the lands and castles of the English in Wales. Almost before he knew it, he was leading a general Welsh rebellion and met with much success. He was proclaimed Prince of Wales and in 1401 attacked Harlech. The attack was beaten off when more English soldiers arrived to help the garrison.

In 1404 Glendower again attacked Harlech. The English garrison in the castle thought the commander, William Hunt, was going to surrender Harlech to the Welsh. So they seized Hunt and imprisoned him. Disease and desertion began to weaken these defenders and finally the garrison was reduced to 20 men. At this point Glendower got the English defenders of the castle to surrender by giving them a sum of money. This, incidentally, was not an uncommon procedure when a castle's garrison thought they had done their duty but were on the verge of being defeated.

Glendower then made Harlech his capital, summoned a parliament to meet there, and used it as his family home. In 1408, however, the English laid siege to Harlech with a force of 1,000 men and subdued it, taking Glendower's wife among the prisoners. As the war went against him, Glendower fled to the mountains, which are many and rugged in Wales. No one really knows what became of him, except that he probably died in 1416. Though this last attempt to establish Welsh independence failed, it turned out that one of Glendower's cousins founded the family from which Henry VII, the first Tudor King of England, was descended.

By the end of the fifteenth century castles like Harlech were no longer of great importance for their original military purposes. In some cases they came to be used as jails for criminals and debtors. Parts of most of the castles had become ruined through lack of care. By the sixteenth century all the buildings in the inner ward at Harlech were completely ruined, and three of the four corner towers were roofless. The northeast tower was still roofed because it was used as a jail and was now known as the Debtor's Tower. The gatehouse was roofed and was used as the judges' lodgings when court sessions were held at Harlech during the reign of Queen Elizabeth I.

Harlech was attacked and defended just once more after the famous siege of 1468. That was in the Puritan Revolution, near the middle of the seventeenth century, when the king and his followers were fighting the Puritans under Oliver Cromwell for control of the British government. Harlech was held for the king by Colonel William Owen and successfully withstood one siege by Cromwell's forces, but a year later it had to surrender.

Much of Harlech Castle still stands today, looking down from its height on the Welsh country and the sea. It is a roofless and floorless ruin, which perhaps is not surprising after almost seven centuries, but it can be visited and examined, and it is still an inspiring memorial to the history of Wales.

One enters Harlech from Castle Green across a modern causeway over the moat to the main gatehouse. The Ministry of Works of the British Government, which now has custody of the castle, recommends that visitors climb the Garden Tower first. This is the name now given the tower on the southeast corner. From this tower one can walk around the top of the walls, past the Weathercock Tower on the southwest and the Chapel Tower on the northwest to the Prison, or Debtor's Tower. In doing this a person gets a fine idea of the general plan of one of these great Edwardian castles. The Garden and Prison Towers each has a round dungeon, lighted by narrow slits, and originally entered by a trap door from the room above.

This story of just one castle of the hundreds that were built in Great Britain shows the important part castles have played in the history of the country. The same thing is true of many other countries. Castles such as Harlech are not just great buildings of stone. Nor are they something out of a fairy tale or a make-believe story of knights and war. They were erected for very practical purposes at the order of kings and nobles, and by the work of many ordinary people. The struggles to defend and capture them were not just meaningless battles started for the honor of individual knights and the love of beautiful ladies. Rather, castles were the scenes of noble and ignoble deeds that expressed the desires and purposes of nations and important people in those nations.

II   The First Castles

LONG BEFORE MEN built such imposing structures as Harlech Castle, they constructed other simpler fortifications. In fact, men have always built some kind of fortification to protect themselves, their families, and their tribes against danger, whether from animals or from other men. The caveman's cave could be used for defense. In prehistoric times, as scientists can tell from ruins they have discovered, men used hills or ledges, and piles of earth and stone to make fortified places to defend themselves against their enemies. Usually they did not live in such places, but only gathered there when danger threatened.

The first great civilizations, around 6,000 years ago in Mesopotamia, protected themselves with fortifications. There, in the Near East, the cities had walls of sun-dried brick. Around 1200 B.C. the city of Troy in what is now Turkey was besieged by the Greeks. As Homer tells the story in the *Iliad,* the Greeks were unable to capture the city because of its strong walls and brave, although outnumbered, defenders. The Greeks finally succeeded by trickery when they constructed an enormous wooden horse which was filled with soldiers. The Trojans, not knowing what was inside, took the horse into their city and were surprised and defeated. Then there is the Bible story of Joshua and the battle of Jericho. The people under Joshua shouted so loud that, as the song says, "the walls came tumbling down" and the town was captured.

The Great Wall of China is perhaps the largest and certainly the longest fortification ever built. It was first constructed over 2,100 years ago and was reconstructed many centuries later. This great stone wall runs for about 1,500 miles across north China, averages 25 feet in height and is from 15 to 30 feet wide. One can judge from this how much material and how much labor, especially in those days before modern machinery, it took to erect the wall. A somewhat similar wall, although not as long, was built by the Romans about 121 to 127 B.C. across the narrow part of the island of Great Britain. It is 73½ miles long and much of it is still preserved today as one of the most impressive remains of the Roman conquest of Britain. It is called Hadrian's Wall after the emperor who had it built. Both the Great Wall of China and Hadrian's Wall were built for protection against invading enemies. From the forts and watch towers placed at intervals along the wall, soldiers could watch for any enemy approaching with the idea of attacking or getting over the walls. The guards on watch could then summon help from other soldiers stationed at various places near the wall.

Fortifications and walled cities have also been built in China, India, and Japan. In the southwestern United States, before the white man came, Indians such as the Pueblos built their communities on mesas and on canyon shelves in order to protect their tribes against others.

Perhaps the best engineers and builders of all time, considering that they did not have the tools, machinery, or means of transportation that we do, were the Romans. Their empire at one time included almost all of Western Europe, and Hadrian's Wall was but one of their many feats. They built bridges, roads, aqueducts, and walls around cities. They also built permanent military camps for their legions which they called *castra*. In the late Roman Empire *castra* were constructed with masonry walls and enclosed about 50 acres. When the Romans built a smaller military strong point of about ten acres, they called it a *castellum* and it is from that Latin word that we get our word castle and the French word *chateau*, which means the same thing.

In the fifth century, barbarians from the eastern and northern parts of Europe began to overrun the Roman Empire. A.D. 476 is the year usually given as the final fall of the Roman Empire. After that there was no longer any one strong, central government that could keep peace and order over a large area. The conquerors of the Romans needed fortified places for protecting themselves, in their own towns or other local areas. But they did not have the skill, experience, or knowledge of the Romans they had defeated and so their forts were not as strong or impressive. They would take an area of about 30 acres, dig a ditch around it, and build up an earthen embankment on the inside of the ditch with a wooden palisade, or wall, on top of it. This might be the headquarters of a prince or an official appointed by him, but no one else lived in it. It was a refuge for the people of the neighborhood, and they all fled to it when an attack was threatened.

Nearly 400 years after the Roman Empire collapsed, there was once again for a short time a fairly strong government in Western Europe. This was when the Emperor Charlemagne ruled, but even he had to rely on many less important princes and nobles to help him. Charlemagne died in A.D. 814, and within 150 years his empire was split up among several of his descendants so that there was no strong power ruling alone over a very large area. This took place mostly in what we now call France and it is there that the first structures that can be called castles were erected.

At that time, 1,000 years ago, small areas, like counties or states, were ruled by nobles. They might be attacked by other nobles, or they might decide they didn't want to do what the king, whom they legally should obey, wanted them to do. So they built a structure that was both a home and a fort. This fortified dwelling place, a private fortress of a noble or a king, was called a castle. The exact date and the place where such a fortification was first built is not known, but it was about 1,000 years ago. The first castles were not very strong or impressive compared with the later castles such as Harlech. They were much smaller in area than the Roman army fortifications, and they were made of earth and wood since the people of those days had

A Motte-and-Bailey Castle

not recaptured the engineering and building skill of the Romans. These early castles are called motte-and-bailey castles.

In building such a castle, the first step was to dig two ditches, more or less circular, and with one larger than the other. The smaller ditch joined into one part of the larger one. The earth that was dug out of the ditches was used to make an earthen embankment on the castle side. Some of the earth was also used to make a high mound in the center of the smaller ditch's circle. If there was a convenient place where the ground was already higher than the surrounding area, that would be the location of this mound, or motte. A wooden wall, or stockade, was built around the whole castle, and the area in the larger circle was called the bailey. Sometimes there would be more than one bailey. There was a bridge across the ditch, leading to a gate into the bailey.

There was also a bridge over the ditch at the rear of the bailey.

This led to the motte, and to a flight of steps up the high earthen bank to the wooden structure on top of the motte. This building, called the keep, was both living quarters for the lord of the castle and the fort that provided the last defense if attackers broke into the bailey. A motte-and-bailey castle had both advantages and disadvantages. It could be built fairly easily and quickly. It gave the people in it an advantage over those attacking because of the protection of its ditch and wall. On the other hand, since the stockades and buildings were of wood, they could be set on fire with torches, and knocked down easier than the later stone walls.

No castles of this kind were erected in England before 1066 but within a few years after that there were several hundred of them. This came about largely through the ambition and effort of one man. He was William, Duke of Normandy, the strong, efficient ruler of a territory that is now part of France. Duke William claimed he should be the next king of England and in 1066 he invaded England with a strong force. Since he was already familiar with the motte-and-bailey castle in Normandy as a useful fortification, one of the first things he did when he landed at Hastings was to build such a castle. With enough men and hard work a motte-and-bailey castle could be put up in six days. In this case, William had even brought with him from Normandy the timber parts and the pegs to fasten them together. The remains of the mound of this castle at Hastings can still be seen, but the other parts of the castle now there are of a later date.

At the Battle of Hastings, William defeated King Harold and the English and soon conquered all of England. The final submission of the English to the Normans came at Berkhampstead, and there William built another castle of which some ruins can be seen today. The motte was about 45 feet high and about 60 feet across at the top. Here the bailey was oblong in shape and measured about 450 by 300 feet. The ditch, or moat, was filled with water. At some castles the motte was higher than this, the one at Thetford Castle, in Norfolk, being 80 feet high.

Duke William was soon crowned King William of England and proceeded to reward his followers. He gave them land and manors that had belonged to the English so that each, subject to the king's direction, ruled over a certain area. To control the still angry and disgruntled Englishmen, William made sure that these lords of his built castles to protect themselves and to house soldiers who could keep order in the surrounding countryside. No one is now sure just how many motte-and-bailey castles were erected in England, but there may have been as many as 500.

One of the most interesting records of the life of William the Conqueror is also a beautiful work of art. It is the Bayeux Tapestry, still preserved at Bayeux in Normandy. According to tradition it was made by William's wife, Queen Matilda, and her handmaidens, but it may actually be of somewhat later origin and have been done by English embroiderers. The tapestry is a strip of coarse linen, 230 feet long and only 20 inches wide. It is embroidered in worsteds of eight colors, and the scenes on it make a valuable historical record. It shows Duke William capturing the castles of Dol, Rennes, and Dinant, and depicts the building of Hastings Castle.

By the twelfth century castles were common in England and on the continent of Europe, and were an important part of the feudal system of government. They were a result of the development of this system, and they were one of the things that kept the system going. Like any system of government, feudalism affected the way people lived, the way they made a living, and their relations with other people and other countries. Castles were a part of this way of life and to understand the part they played, it is necessary to know something about feudalism, with its ideals of chivalry and knighthood.

III   Chivalry, Knighthood, and Castles

WHENEVER ANYTHING IS written about knights, or chivalry, or castles, or the Middle Ages, the word feudal or the phrase feudal system is sure to appear. It is easier to understand what the feudal system was if one starts with the word itself. From an old Germanic word meaning cattle or property, there came the Latin word *feodum*, and from that came the words feudal and feudalism.

The feudal system was based on relationships between people which, in turn, determined their rights and property. In Western Europe, from the ninth century into the fifteenth century, feudalism was the system of government and the way people lived in their relations with each other. The system was not called feudalism then, but that is the name historians later gave to it. It began when strong central governments broke down, so that officials and nobles in small areas became powerful and important. At the same time there grew up new kinds of personal relationships between kings and various degrees of nobles. Kings, princes, dukes, and counts gave certain rights to less important nobles in return for their support, and this created a whole way of life that determined how everyone lived, from the king to the poorest serf, or peasant.

Feudalism differed greatly from the strong empire, ruled from Rome by the emperor and his court and army, which had preceded it. Eventually, it also came to an end when kings in the various European countries became strong enough again to rule over countries of the size we know today. During the 500 or so years that the feudal system existed, it included the customs and practices called chivalry and knighthood. Castles and their builders, owners, and defenders played a very important part in the system.

Two other key words in understanding the feudal system are vassalage and fief-holding. Vassalage was an honorable and personal relationship between two men of the ruling class. A duke, for example, would become the vassal of a king. The king, who owned all or most of the land in the country, could confer authority and lands upon the duke. The king, on his part, needed the support of dukes and other nobles in war and in ruling the country. The noble would appear before the king and kneel in front of him. Placing his hands between those of the king, the noble would acknowledge that he was the king's vassal and pledge his faith to him against all men. The king would then accept the noble's pledge, raise him to his feet, and kiss him. This act by the noble was called homage. Then the noble, on the Gospels or some sacred relic, took a solemn oath to live up to his earlier promises. This was the oath of fealty.

The acts of homage and fealty created an arrangement that was of mutual advantage to the king and the noble. The king gave certain authority to the noble to rule within his territory and promised to protect him. Usually he also granted a fief, which meant he gave the noble the use of a certain piece of land. It was here that the vassal governed from a castle. There was almost none of today's business, manufacturing, or commerce. The serfs tilled the land on the noble's fief, or manor, and gave part of the crops, as well as their labor on other projects, to the noble in return for his protection and the right to farm the land.

The noble, in turn, promised to support the king in any way and to supply knights to help fight for the king. Usually the arrangement was specific as to just how many knights and how many days a year they had to serve the king. Sometimes the knights or other soldiers had to be supplied to defend one of the king's castles.

The most powerful nobles, the dukes, the earls, and the counts, often held several fiefs and they in turn accepted lesser nobles as their vassals and granted them the same rights in some of their lands that they had received from the king. Thus, when the king called on a very important noble for the knights he had promised, that nobleman in turn called on his own vassals to supply the fighting men they had promised. It was in this way that a general system of government was established throughout a country and that armies were raised when there was a war. The various nobles, all of them trained to be warriors, lived on the lands granted them by the lord next above, up to the king himself. They ruled the lives of all the people on their land. Nearly everyone helped in farming and, for the most part, food and clothing materials came from the manor lands around the castle.

During the feudal era, and growing out of its system of personal relationships between people of greater and lesser standing, there arose the idea of chivalry and the ideals it stood for. Chivalry, originating in France and Spain and spreading to the rest of the continent and to England, was strongest in the twelfth and thirteenth centuries. Again, as with feudalism, the meaning of chivalry is clearer when the word itself is traced back. In French, *cheval* means horse, and a man who was of the noble class, who could afford one or more horses (which were rather scarce and expensive in those days), and was trained to fight as a cavalryman, was a *chevalier*. Such people built up the customs, habits, and ideals of chivalry.

In this code of behavior the chief virtues were piety, bravery, loyalty, and honor. The people of Western Europe were by this time Christians. Everything they did was done in the name of the Christian God, and the church exercised considerable influence over the conduct of knights and other members of the noble, military class. Above all, a warrior knight was expected to be brave, no matter what the odds against him in battle, and to be completely loyal to his master— a higher noble, or the king himself. Perhaps the best example of this is in the French epic poem, the *Song of Roland*. According to the poem, the rearguard of Charlemagne's army was exposed to attack by the Saracens through treachery. Roland, refusing to summon help and loyal to the emperor to the end, charged the enemy with those who would follow him although he knew it meant certain death. His honor would not let him go back on his oath to his king.

Chivalry helped lessen the harshness of the warfare of the time, for emphasis was laid on the courteous treatment of prisoners. Even so, kings and nobles were held for ransom when captured, and the code of chivalry applied only between members of the noble, ruling class. They did not have to apply this code to the common people under them. The chief occupation of the nobles was warfare, so they seem to have thought nothing of the violence and bloodshed that accompanied it. A warrior was supposed to fight as hard as he could, and it was perfectly proper to burn the homes of the enemy and seize his possessions. The whole idea of chivalry in warfare implied nothing more than the respect of one warrior for another. In fact, warfare between nobles became so fierce that at one time in the Middle Ages the church attempted to limit such private battles. Fighting was prohibited from Wednesday or Thursday evening until Monday morning and on certain religious holidays. Excommunication from the church was the punishment for those who violated the truce. This was called the Truce of God.

A knight of the Middle Ages could be defined as a member of the nobility who was trained and armed as a warrior on horseback. Almost without exception he had to be born a member of the noble class, but that did not make him a knight. He had to earn this rank through long and hard training. He began to learn to ride a horse and to use arms almost as soon as he could walk. During his younger years he would be called in France a *valet*, which meant a little vassal, and in England a page.

When he was about 14 he got a new title—squire. After that he was attached to a knight and accompanied him and assisted him. In battle, the squire carried the knight's reserve of arms and led his extra horse, if he had one. He helped put on the knight's armor, and aided him if he was wounded. In time of peace, he practiced with all the weapons of the day and fought sham battles with other squires. Finally, when he was well-trained and especially if he had already proved himself a warrior in battle, he was rewarded with knighthood.

There was a special ceremony for this, and a solemn one it was. Usually the ceremony was performed by the boy's father, or by his overlord. The new knight was presented with arms and was given the "accolade," a blow on the neck or shoulders, delivered either with the hand or the flat of a sword. In the later days of feudalism, this ceremony was preceded by a night-long vigil before a church altar. In some cases, a squire who showed particular bravery was made a knight right on the field of battle. In Great Britain men are still made knights, although usually for services other than military, and there is still a ceremony at which the king or queen "dubs" a person a knight by touching him on the shoulder with a sword.

A knight was a full-fledged warrior and a member of the ruling class. Then, or when he succeeded his father, he would be a vassal of some higher lord. He would probably hold a fief, which for the more important noble knights included a castle. He was obligated to fight for the king or his overlord, to help garrison a castle, or to see to it that the lesser knights under him served the king or garrisoned a castle when ordered to do so in accordance with their sworn promises.

When not engaged in actual warfare, knights often took part in tournaments. These might be called a combination of our present-day track and field meets and military maneuvers. At first they were battles in a very real sense, except that they were planned in advance and there were rules agreed upon. Toward the end of the twelfth and into the early thirteenth century a tournament was a serious and bloody affair between two groups of knights. If lances were broken, combat was continued with swords. The victor could claim the horse and arms of his opponent unless the latter ransomed them for a sum of money. It was good training for soldiers in a way, but it was dangerous. Later, the tournaments became somewhat more like boxing or fencing matches, so that skill was tested, but actual injuries with sword and lance were not inflicted. Often such affairs were held in an open space in front of a castle.

31

As time went on there came to be more knights than there were castles or fiefs for them to rule and to get a living from. A noble might have several sons who became knights, but usually only the eldest inherited the land or became the next vassal to hold the fief. After the Crusades began, when the nobility of Europe tried to win back the Holy Land from the Saracens, these knights and others formed themselves into some famous orders of knighthood. The first of these were the Knights Templars, organized to defend pilgrims traveling to Jerusalem. They were called this because they established their headquarters in a house near Solomon's Temple. The Knights Hospitalers were a similar order. When Palestine was retaken by the Turks, they went to Cyprus and then conquered the island of Rhodes where they remained for 200 years. Later they retreated to the island of Malta where they withstood the attacks of the Turks and became known as the Knights of Malta.

The castle is a fine symbol of the age of chivalry and knighthood. Once again, the history of a word shows this as well as anything can. The word used for the part of the castle in which the lord dwelt was, in French, *donjon*. (In English this became dungeon, but it was only later that the word came to mean a dark, sinister prison.) The word *donjon* is derived from the Latin *dominum*, which expresses lordship. The holder of the castle was a member of the aristocracy, which was a purely military class. He ruled the lands dominated by his castle, so long as he was faithful to the higher lord whose vassal he was—or until some more powerful noble was able to besiege and capture the castle.

The castle was both a home and a fortress for the ruling lord. From it, with his own retainers and knights who owed service to him, he could rule his territory. The farm lands around the castle provided him with food and clothing. The castles, by the way they were situated on high ground or overlooking river crossings, and by the people dependent on them, determined who ruled a particular part of a country.

The great importance of castles was taken into account in the feudal system and in the relationships brought about by vassalage. First of all, all castles, in a sense, belonged to the king. At least, castles were not supposed to be built without his permission, although in some countries at some periods the great nobles were so powerful that they could defy the king and do as they pleased. A king was anxious to have powerful lords on his side and to make sure that they built and kept in repair strong castles in their lands. At the same time, though, if a noble became strong and controlled one or more great castles, he might be tempted to turn against the king and defy him. In part, then, the Middle Ages was a constant struggle between the king, representing a central government, and nobles who wanted to do as they pleased in their own territories. In all such struggles, castles played key parts as the only great military defenses of the period.

One of the duties of those who held fiefs was to furnish castle guards, knights and other soldiers to garrison a castle, because a castle had to be able to defend itself at all times. A knight, as part of his fief, might be required to help guard a castle of the noble over him, or of the king himself. For instance, the Earls of Richmond required about 30 knights to serve in their castle every two months. In another case a group of knights took turns, ten of them serving to garrison a castle of the King of England for three months at a time. Later, kings and great barons accepted money in place of special services and then used the money to hire soldiers to guard their castles. In the twelfth century in England, the normal rate for hiring a knight to perform such service was six or eight pence a day.

These are but a few examples of the rules and customs of the feudal era concerning castles. They help show the important place castles held in the whole system, and it is no wonder, then, that for hundreds of years great effort was expended to make castles bigger and stronger.

IV   The Age of the Great Castles

WHETHER IN SPORTS or in warfare, any idea that improves the situation of the offense almost at once stimulates the defense to think up ways of meeting the new threat. When the T-formation in football was first introduced, the offense—the team with the ball—had a great advantage, and the defense found it very difficult to stop its opponent from scoring. Immediately, coaches and players began thinking and experimenting, and soon came up with ways of meeting the new system of attack.

The same thing has happened many times in warfare and perhaps no more dramatically than in the problem of attacking and defending a castle. In this case, the defenders managed to keep the advantage for nearly 400 years. As a result, some of the most impressive and magnificent structures ever erected by man are the castles of the Middle Ages. The fact that many hundreds of them still exist, even though partly in ruins, is the best testimony to their success.

When the first castles were built, about 1,000 years ago, most of them were rather simple constructions of earth and wood, although some used stone if such material was readily available. Very soon, the nobles and soldiers found that the wooden walls could be set on fire quite easily. The ditches and the earthen walls were neither very deep nor very high, and a concerted rush by resolute attackers could sweep over them and capture the castle and its defenders. Also, men began devising better weapons for attacking castles—instruments for firing large stones and ways of hurling fire at the walls.

They also developed new methods for protecting themselves when they advanced against the arrows of the defenders.

The builders of castles were thus stimulated to make them more difficult to capture. First of all, they began to use stone instead of wood and earth. They made the ditches wider and deeper and filled them with water. They built the walls higher; they built towers at the corners; and they built two walls, an outer and an inner "curtain." They began to make even better use of topography, that is, the lay of the land. They erected the castles on high points, where they overlooked a large area of the countryside and where steep cliffs made it difficult, if not impossible, for attackers to get at the castle from one or more sides. Often, too, this high point commanded a narrow pass through hills or mountains, or stood just above a river so that no one could go up and down it in boats unless the noble who owned the castle allowed them to do so.

Perhaps the greatest influence on castle building in Western Europe and the stimulus that resulted in the great and powerful medieval castles was the Crusades. The Crusades were a series of wars undertaken by European Christians to reconquer the Holy Land in the Near East from the Moslem people who had come to rule that region. Although the warfare between the Crusaders and the Moslem world went on more or less continually for about 200 years, the main efforts were divided into nine Crusades. The first began in 1095 and lasted until 1099.

The Crusaders were surprised at what they found. They discovered that in some ways the Moslems were ahead of them—in scientific knowledge, in some of the comforts of life, and in their skill at building military fortifications. The ancestors of the Crusaders had brought about the fall of the Roman Empire in Western Europe, but they had been so intent on doing so, and so behind in technology and education, that they did not appreciate the achievements of the Romans. Consequently, they did not copy or try to learn from the Romans, one of whose greatest skills had been that of building fortresses. So they had to start all over again, as they had done with

35

Krak des Chevaliers, Syria

wood and earth castles and with almost no knowledge of machines and methods that would help them build bigger and stronger buildings.

But the Crusaders found that the Moslem rulers had wisely studied the Roman buildings and fortifications which had been built in the Near East. The Moslems had not been so anxious to destroy everything the Romans had done, but had copied the buildings and building methods. In fact, as early as the eighth century, Moslem rulers had erected palaces which resembled the purely military forts of the Romans on the outside but were, for those times, luxurious palaces inside.

The Crusaders did two things. They began to build enormously strong stone castles in those parts of the Holy Land which they were able to capture, and they took back to Europe the knowledge of how to erect such structures. One of the most famous castles of all time is that of Krak des Chevaliers, or Castle of the Knights, which the Crusaders built in what is now Syria. The Knights Hospitalers began the castle in 1131, and it still stands today in an excellent state of preservation as one of the masterpieces of medieval military architecture. It rises on a lonely vantage point, among bare mountains, and by its position dominates both the north-south and the east-west routes of that part of Syria.

This castle was as strong in its day as it looks even now. It has a double line of walls around it, with great round towers, underground passages, and even a somberly beautiful chapel. The steep banks leading up to its walls were enough to discourage any attacker. One of the important points about castles of this type is that they are concentric, that is, all the defenses have a common center so that the castle is equally able to withstand an attack from any direction. This is in contrast to the early motte-and-bailey castle with its less heavily defended baileys.

One of the Crusaders who brought back to Europe new knowledge about castle building was Richard I of England, also known as Richard Coeur de Lion, or Richard the Lion-Hearted. He was the perfect example of the king of the age of chivalry, and every reader of Sir Walter Scott's *Ivanhoe* knows of his knightly exploits. Unfortunately for the people of England he was too busy with the Crusades and other adventures to give much thought to the government of his country, but his military career helps trace the development of castles in Europe in the late twelfth century.

Richard, with the two other great kings of Europe of the time—the German Emperor Frederick I and King Philip II of France—led the Third Crusade which began in 1189. In the Holy Land he was easily the most dashing leader and fought against the forces of the Saracen ruler Saladin. Although Richard was leading the Christian forces against what the Crusaders called the infidels, he discovered that Saladin was a man much like himself, and the two came to respect each other as honorable men and soldiers, despite

37

their bitter conflict. On his way home, Richard was captured and imprisoned in Durnstein Castle by Leopold II, Margrave of Austria, and was released only after the English people paid a huge ransom for their king.

As Duke of Normandy as well as King of England, Richard came into conflict with the King of France, and in 1196 he used his knowledge and experience in the Holy Land to build the most perfect fortress he could devise. He called it Chateau Gaillard, or Saucy Castle, and once described it as "my beautiful one-year-old daughter." It stood above the Seine River at Les Andelys in northwestern France, guarding a gateway to Normandy. Richard personally supervised the building of the castle which included the most advanced ideas of the day. It was rather long and narrow, because of the way the land lay, and was guarded partly by steep slopes, partly by great walls and moats. This castle had not one but three baileys, with the keep in the inner and strongest bailey.

Richard thought it was the strongest castle in the world. Philip, King of France, said that "if its walls were iron I would take it." Richard, his bitter enemy by now, replied: "If they were of butter I would hold it." The test between the two men never came about because Richard was killed in 1199, when he was only 42 years old. He was besieging a small, weak castle when, riding too near the walls, he was struck by a bolt shot from a crossbow and died of the wound. Five years later King Philip made good his boast by capturing Chateau Gaillard, although he had to starve the defenders into submission rather than take the castle by assault. Almost 400 years later, when castles were much less important in warfare, Henry IV of France had Gaillard's defenses dismantled, but it is still an impressive and exciting sight, one of the great memorials of the age of castles.

The development of castles, from the simple motte-and-bailey type already described, to the great structures such as Chateau Gaillard and Harlech Castle, can be traced through two other styles of building. One of these is called the rectangular keep and the other

Chateau Gaillard, France

the shell keep. Both of these developed out of the motte-and-bailey, a few of them at about the same time that the latter was being constructed in large numbers. In turn, the rectangular and shell-keep type of castle gave way to the concentric castle, with round towers and higher and stronger walls that resulted from knowledge gained in the Crusades and from the necessity of defending against increasingly powerful weapons.

The rectangular keeps, or towers, are still among the most imposing relics of the Middle Ages, especially in England. They were an improvement in stone of the wooden keeps erected on the mounds in early castle building. Usually, though, because of their weight they could not be built on the earlier earthen mound. To compensate for this, they were constructed with the only entrance at the second floor. Like the older wooden keeps, they were the last defense and were surrounded by a curtain wall. These rectangular keeps had their greatest development in Britain in the twelfth century during the reign of Henry II. Many castles had been built during the reign of his predecessor, King Stephen, and Henry destroyed them, building in their place these imposing great towers. He saw to it that they remained in his hands.

Although none of these towers was exactly alike, they were much the same. They were taller than they were wide or long. The ground floor was for storage, and living accommodations were above it. Access to the entrance was by a stairway, which often was enclosed in a smaller outer building. This building or the keep itself would have a chapel. The keep would have a well, and facilities for cooking, although usually there was not a real kitchen. On the whole, accommodations were rather crude. Such structures were built more for defense than for comfort, although as time went on they became more comfortable and luxurious.

In the shell-keep type of castle, more emphasis was placed on the walls as defense, rather than centering the strength in the tower keep. The earlier wooden walls around the summit of the motte gave place to stone, and in turn double rows of walls were built.

The various buildings, for storage and cooking and for housing the people, were built in the courtyard against the inner walls instead of being concentrated in a tower. Many castles were built on the sites of older ones, and each generation improved on the work of its predecessors. As a result, many castles today show different stages of building and strengthening, perhaps over a period of several hundred years. Some of them ended up as a combination of various styles and eras of castle building.

The changes in the way castles were constructed can be seen in many fine examples in England. The best known is the Tower of London, which was begun by William the Conqueror as a stone rectangular keep in 1078 when almost all other castles in England were of wood and earth. The White Tower, as it is now known, is today the center of an area of 18 acres of towers, walls, and moat (now dry), expanded and improved by William's successors on the throne of England. One side of the Tower of London faces on the Thames

The Tower of London, England

Restormel Castle, England

River. For a great number of years the Tower was both a source of power of the rulers of England, many of whom lived there at least part of the time, and a jail for important prisoners. Elizabeth I was confined in the Tower before she became queen.

Restormel Castle in Cornwall is a fine example of the shell-keep type of construction in England. By its position on land that fell steeply on three sides, it was a perfect site for a circular shell with the various buildings constructed around the inside of the wall. As in so many cases, Restormel originally had an earthwork wall with a timber palisade which was replaced near the end of the twelfth century by the stronger stone curtain.

Kenilworth Castle, although now in ruins, is remembered as the setting of Scott's novel *Kenilworth* and is an example of the kind of castle that began as a tower keep and ended up much enlarged and elaborated upon. The keep was erected in the second half of the twelfth century, with a square turret at each angle and walls 20 feet thick at the base. Early in the thirteenth century King John built a wall around the outer court. By digging and damming, the water area that was created around the castle to make it impregnable covered 111 acres. In 1266 King Henry III besieged the castle, then held by the younger Simon de Montfort. It held out from June to December and gave up only when food ran low and disease spread among the defenders. Late in the fourteenth century John of Gaunt erected a great hall against the walls of the inner court which he reconstructed. Other owners and rulers of Kenilworth made other changes and improvements over the centuries, so that what probably began as an earth-and-timber fortress in the early twelfth century was changed, improved, and reconstructed for about 400 years. In 1575 Robert Dudley, Earl of Leicester, entertained Queen Elizabeth I who had given him the castle. These lavish "princely pleasures," described by Scott, are said to have cost £60,000.

Kenilworth Castle, England

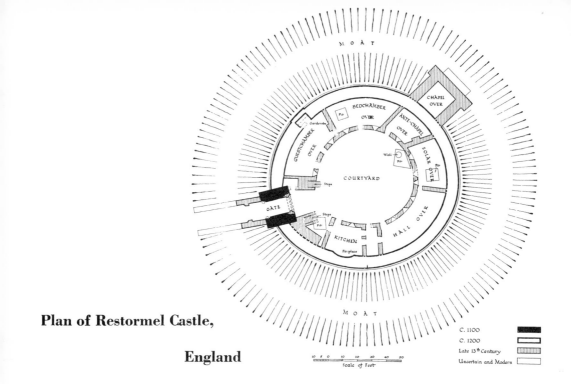

Plan of Restormel Castle,

England

C. 1100

C. 1200

Late 13th Century

Uncertain and Modern

10 5 0   10   20   30   40   50
Scale of Feet

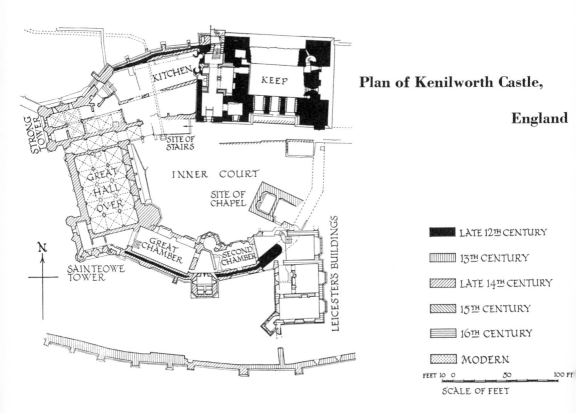

Plan of Kenilworth Castle,

England

LATE 12TH CENTURY

13TH CENTURY

LATE 14TH CENTURY

15TH CENTURY

16TH CENTURY

MODERN

FEET 10 0   50   100 FT

SCALE OF FEET

The largest inhabited castle in the world is Windsor Castle, about 20 miles from London, which for over 800 years has been the home of English monarchs. It was begun by William the Conqueror in the late eleventh century. In size and plan it has not been changed basically since, although many rulers have extended and altered it. It is about 630 by 180 yards, comprising two wards, or baileys. In 1348 Edward III founded the Order of the Garter, one of the highest honors any Englishman can receive, at Windsor. Edward IV in the late fifteenth century began building St. George's Chapel, a beautiful structure dedicated to the patron saint of the order. Many British rulers are buried at Windsor, including every monarch since George III.

Castle building in England reached its peak in the late thirteenth century when Edward I built such castles as Harlech, described in the first chapter. One most important change came in this century. The towers which had been built square became circular, or D-shaped, so that the part projecting out from the walls presented a rounded surface to attackers. The circular tower was introduced into England at a time when keeps, as a last resort of the defenders, were still of value. As a result there are a small number of circular keeps, identical except in shape with the square keeps already described. By this time, though, castle builders were concentrating on strengthening the walls, and were beginning to abandon the idea of the keep entirely.

These strong walls gave better protection to the people inside the castle. They also gave the defenders a much greater area over which they could fire on the attackers. The walls became higher, so that they were harder to scale. From the circular towers jutting out from the walls, the defenders could fire on attackers along the wall as well as on the enemy directly in front of them. Finally, the circular towers were stronger, not having the weakness of the square corners of older towers. They could not be destroyed as easily by enemy attackers seeking to mine underneath and cause the walls and towers to collapse. At first the round towers were made solid, but soon they were built hollow. This gave additional accommodations for those in the castle

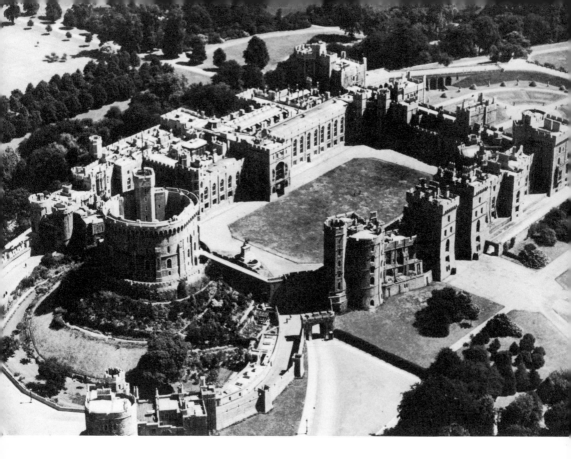

Windsor Castle, England

and provided more platforms from which to fight.

The other parts of the British Isles—Scotland and Ireland—have interesting and historic castles, too. A familiar landmark in Scotland's capital is Edinburgh Castle, on Castle Rock, about 400 feet high, overlooking Princes Street. As far back as the early seventh century, King Edwin of Northumbria occupied this site and erected some kind of fort. The medieval castle surrendered to King Henry II of England in 1174. In 1313 the rock was scaled on its steepest side by the Earl of Moray and 30 followers, who astonished the English garrison and seized the castle for the Scottish King, Robert the Bruce.

Here in Edinburgh Castle in 1566 a son was born to Mary Queen of Scots. He later became King James VI of Scotland and James I of England. A few years later, in 1573, the castle surrendered, after much damage, to the enemies of Mary.

Edinburgh Castle, Scotland

Glamis Castle, Scotland

At Stirling is another castle on a summit above a city, which long rivaled Edinburgh as a royal residence. The castle was captured by the English under Edward I in 1304 after a three months siege, but ten years later it was retaken by the Scots after the Battle of Bannockburn. King James II was born in Stirling Castle.

At Dunbar, east of Edinburgh, are the remains of a castle first built in 1072. It was held for six weeks in 1339 against the English by a Countess of Dunbar who was known as "Black Agnes." In 1567, a man named Bothwell seized Mary Queen of Scots, carried her off to this castle, and married her. The next year the castle was dismantled.

Glamis Castle is traditionally associated with Macbeth who, in Shakespeare's play, murdered Duncan, King of Scotland, here in the eleventh century. Since the fourteenth century Glamis has belonged to the Lyon family and it was the childhood home of Lady Elizabeth Bowes-Lyon who married George VI of England and became the mother of the present Queen Elizabeth II.

Ireland has its historical castles, such as Dublin, built about 1200. To the Irish it was the symbol of English influence for many, many years as the residence of the Lords Lieutenant of Ireland until 1922. At Kilkenny, the city that gave its name to the Kilkenny cats who tore each other apart, there is a fortress above the Nore River. It was begun in the twelfth century by an Englishman known as Richard Strongbow, whose real name was Richard de Clare, second Earl of

Kilkenny Castle, Ireland

Pembroke. He went to Ireland in 1170 and subdued much of the country. In the thirteenth century the present castle was built on the same site. At Limerick, which must somehow have given its name to the well-known verse form, a Norman style castle was started in 1210 when King John visited Limerick. It dominated the crossing of the River Shannon.

In Northern Ireland is a fine old castle, Carrickfergus, now preserved as a monument of its times. It was built in 1178 and was for several centuries an Anglo-Norman garrison headquarters. King John in 1210 had to hasten here to put down a rebellion, and the room which he is said to have occupied is still known as King John's Room.

The British Isles thus can boast of excellent examples of castles of all kinds and ages, but other countries have many interesting and important castles also.

V More Great Castles

SINCE THE CONDITIONS of life and the system of government were much the same in all of Western Europe in the Middle Ages, many castles were built in the countries on the continent as well as in England. Hundreds of castles of all different periods were erected in such countries as France, Spain, Italy, Germany, Austria, Switzerland, Belgium, and Denmark. In each country there were certain differences because of history, or temperament, or the kind of government. On the whole, though, there is the same story of development and change, and the same imposing and romantic ruins can be seen, telling their stories of bygone times and long dead kings, and lords, and knights.

France is a land of many old and beautiful castles. The French word for castle, *chateau*, has in fact come to mean a large, handsome mansion or country house. Along the River Loire, in particular, are the remains of many castles, perched on hills, or located on river banks at strategic points.

At Angers, the capital of Anjou, which was one of the great duchies of France in the Middle Ages, there is a powerful castle, reconstructed as it is now by King Louis IX about 1230. Its great bare walls rise from massive bases. The famed Fulk Nerra lived here, and after him the Plantagenets, who were then counts of Anjou and later kings of England. Fulk Nerra was Count of Anjou from 987 to 1040 and fought regularly with his neighbors of Brittany, Blois, and Touraine. He built castles and attacked and captured others. Although the tops

51

of the towers were later changed, the great fortress of Angers once exhibited the typical French tower tops—the conical style that made them look like witches' hats. Angers Castle is five-sided like the Pentagon Building.

Angers Castle, France

Saumur Castle, France

Saumur Castle tops an isolated crag where, about a thousand years ago, the Count of Blois and Touraine, known as Thibaut the Trickster, first built a fortress. Fulk Nerra captured it in 1026, and it was reconstructed at the end of the fourteenth century in such a way that it took on a much more splendid appearance than it had had in the days when it was strictly a military stronghold. Saumur thus shows the changes from feudal to Renaissance architecture. Photographs of Saumur as it is today can be compared with a famous work of art that is over 400 years old. In the early fifteenth century three brothers, Pol, Hennequin, and Hermann de Limbourg, were employed by John, Duke of Berry. They made a great, handsome book called

Saumur Castle, France (from the "Très Riches Heures"*)*

the *Très Riches Heures*. It contained 39 illustrations of country life including Saumur Castle as it looked to them.

In northern France is Coucy Castle, which had a bad name in the twelfth century because of the kind of barons who held it. They were called robber barons because they used their castle and their power to hold up and rob travelers in their territory. Unfortunately for travelers, there were quite a few such castle-owning nobles in the Middle Ages. On the other hand, one of the lords of Coucy, Guy II who died about 1203, was a famous poet and singer—a troubadour. Coucy Castle was damaged in World War I.

In southeastern France, in Provence and on the Rhone River, are two interesting castles. One is at Tarascon, built by order of Good King René to keep guard over the river. The other is at Avignon which was the residence of the Popes from 1309 to 1377. They built a large structure on top of a hill which perhaps is not a castle in the strict sense of the word, but is a building well worth seeing—a residence, fortress, and place of worship all in one.

On the Aude River in southern France is another interesting example of medieval military building although, like Avignon, it is more than a castle. This is Carcassonne. The structure, atop a hill, encloses a whole medieval city with walls a mile around. There is a twelfth-century castle within the walls. The outer walls were erected in the thirteenth century, but parts of the inner walls go back as far as the sixth century when the barbarian Visigoth invaders of France built defenses here. Carcassonne was captured in 1209 by Simon de Montfort. In the nineteenth century the French architect Viollet-le-Duc restored the old walled city to something like its medieval glory. Today it stands as one of the architectural marvels of France.

Coucy Castle, France

City of Carcassonne, France

Tarascon Castle, France

Spain has its handsome and imposing castles. Here the word *alcazar* is often used and refers to strong, but not entirely fortress-like, structures that were built inside cities during the centuries of Moslem rule of the country. In addition, there was the palace-fortress type of structure such as the Alhambra, overlooking the city of Granada. Started in the thirteenth century and built chiefly between 1348 and 1354, the buildings of the Alhambra provided the Moorish kings, as the Moslem rulers were called in Spain, with a fortress for defense, a palace for luxurious living, and quarters for various nobles and officials. Alhambra comes from an Arabic word meaning "the red castle." A wall studded with towers surrounds the Alhambra, the greatest monument of Moorish art in Spain. On January 2, 1492, Boabdil, the last of the Moslem princes of Granada, surrendered the city and the Alhambra after a siege. His conquerors were King Ferdinand and Queen Isabella who that same year helped Christopher Columbus launch his sea adventure which resulted in the discovery of America.

There are famous alcazars at Cordoba, Segovia, Seville, and Toledo. The one at Cordoba is now in ruins. The alcazar at Segovia, possibly located on the site of a Roman fortress on steep cliffs, towers over the city where two rivers meet. It was begun in the eleventh century, constructed mostly in the fifteenth, and restored in the nineteenth. It was a favorite residence of the kings of Castile, and Isabella I was crowned here.

At Seville the alcazar, erected by the Moors in the twelfth century, was rebuilt and enlarged in the fourteenth century by a king known as Peter the Cruel. The alcazar of Toledo, standing on the highest peak of a city built on hills, is probably the best-known structure of its kind. Originally, it too was a Moorish structure. It was restored in the thirteenth century and then in the sixteenth was transformed again to serve as a regal residence for Charles V and Philip II. The great strength of such a fortress was demonstrated in modern times when, despite the power of twentieth-century weapons, it withstood a siege of more than two months, the Loyalists attacking and the

The Alcazar at Segovia, Spain

Insurgents defending it in 1936 during the Spanish Civil War. It was largely destroyed in this battle.

Many other cities of Spain have castles, or ruins of castles, of interest. Alicante has two, the Castle of Santa Barbara and the Castle of San Fernando, each on a steep, isolated hill. La Mota Castle at Valladolid is a very powerful looking structure of the fifteenth century. At Cadiz are San Sebastian and Santa Catalina castles, and at Torija are the remains of a castle of the Knights Templars, famous for their exploits in the Holy Land.

La Mota Castle, Spain

Italy, considering its size and its long history, has fewer real castles than might be expected. This came about because its government in the Middle Ages was organized around the "city-states" rather than the idea of a national king and feudal lords. The Italian nobles ruled from walled cities, or fortress-castles within those cities. Still, there are some interesting examples of Italian contributions to the age of castles.

The troubled times Rome went through, first as a result of barbarian and Saracen invasions and then from internal conflict, resulted in the construction of towers and castles within the city. These were built in the eleventh and twelfth centuries. Instead of starting with new materials, the builders simply used stones from older structures dating from the time of the Roman Empire. The Casa di Rienzi is said to be the oldest remaining example of this medieval domestic architecture in Rome.

Much earlier the first steps were taken to build what is still today a landmark of Rome. It is called the Castel Sant' Angelo, on the right bank of the Tiber. It was originally built about 1800 years ago by the Emperor Hadrian as a tomb for himself and future emperors. It was first made into a fortress by the military commander Belisarius when the Goths besieged Rome. It has been much changed through the centuries and has frequently been a place of refuge for the Popes because it was connected to the Vatican by a secret passage. It was used as a fortress and prison until 1870.

At Verona the powerful Scaligeri family that ruled the city for more than 100 years in the thirteenth and fourteenth centuries built a castle to help maintain their power. These rulers of Verona are good examples of the tough nobles who governed the city-states of Italy and fought with other noble families of other cities—or even within their own city. The Scaligeri family were leaders of the Ghibelline faction, which was at almost continuous war throughout much of Italy with other nobles who made up the Guelph party. This history of faction, city, and noble enmity was used by Shakespeare when he made Verona the setting for "Romeo and Juliet," although he

Castle of the Scaligeri, Italy

Ursino Castle, Sicily

changed the family names to Montague and Capulet.

Naples has three castles: dell' Ovo, Sant' Elmo, and Nuovo. Sant' Elmo was built in the fourteenth century on a dominating hill more than 800 feet high. Charles I of Anjou built Nuovo between 1279 and 1284. Leghorn began chiefly as a castle built as a defense against the Saracens and later, under the Medici, developed into a flourishing city. Milan has one of the most magnificent of Italian castles, the fifteenth-century Castello Sforzesco, erected by the Sforza family after they became the rulers of the city. On the island of Sicily at Catania there is Ursino Castle, built in 1232 by the Emperor Frederick II, and at Palermo two castles, La Zisa and La Cuba, which show the work of those famous enemies, the Normans and the Saracens.

Among Germany's many impressive castles, the best known is probably Heidelberg, on the Neckar River in the western part of the country. Although now in ruins, it was a magnificent structure of red sandstone, started in the thirteenth century and enlarged considerably between the fifteenth and seventeenth centuries. Heidelberg towers above the famous university city of the same name. In the castle cellar is the Heidelberg Tun, a gigantic wine cask that will hold 58,650 gallons.

Heidelberg Castle,

Germany

At Cleves, also in western Germany, is the eleventh-century castle of Schwanenburg. Its name means "swan's castle" and it is associated with the legend of Lohengrin. In a German story of the Middle Ages, Lohengrin, a knight of the Grail, was sent to rescue a princess named Elsa. Led by a swan, he found her and married her. The princess had been warned that she should not ask her husband's name, but she did, and this meant he had to return to the castle of the Grail. Then the swan reappeared and turned out to be Elsa's brother. The great composer Richard Wagner used this story for his opera "Lohengrin," although the setting of the opera is Antwerp, Belgium.

In southern Germany near Lake Constance is the castle of the Hohenzollerns. From it a princely family, which can be traced back to the eleventh century, took this name. Over the centuries the area of their rule increased and from 1871 to 1918 they were the emperors of the Germany that was so powerful until the end of World War I.

At Schwangau are two castles, the one of this name having been built only about 100 years ago, which means that it isn't a true castle in the sense of such a structure erected in medieval times. The castle of Hohenschwangau, on the other hand, is an ancient and true castle. Kronberg Castle is old but was rebuilt and restored only 60 years ago. Harburg is mostly a seventeenth-century castle, but it has a thirteenth-century watchtower. Among the many other German castles are Falkenburg, Georghausen, Guttenberg, Munzenberg, Reichenberg, Schonburg, and Thierstein.

Most of the castles just mentioned are in western or southern Germany. As a result of the activities of one of the famous orders of knights, other castles and fortresses were built in eastern Germany and in Poland. This was the organization known as the Teutonic Knights, a religious and military order founded in 1190 to help take care of the sick and wounded during the siege of Acre in the Third Crusade. About 1225 the Teutonic Knights moved to eastern Europe when they were called to crusade against the then heathen Prussians. They subdued them and built fortresses. By 1309 they established

Castle of the Hohenzollerns, Germany

their headquarters in the castle of Marienburg, near the Vistula River in what is now Poland.

Austria is a small country, but it has a long history, and is another land in which castles played a prominent part for many centuries. Even today Austria claims about 1,000 castles well enough preserved to live in and another 600 crumbling strongholds and ruins. Hainburg Castle on the Danube is very ancient as a fortification. Prince Leopold V was able to develop it into the strongest fortress east of Vienna by using some of the ransom money the English paid to free their captive king, Richard the Lion-Hearted. Another great stronghold is Hochosterwitz Castle, near Klagenfurt. This castle was first built in the late ninth century, but its great period was from 1570 to 1586 when it was strengthened against the threatened onslaught of the Turks. It had several rings of walls, 14 towers, and was on a high rocky hill. It was so strong that it was never besieged, let alone captured.

During the invasion of the Turks into Austria in the seventeenth century, 11,000 civilians took refuge in Starhemberg Castle, in addition to the several thousand soldiers there, showing how large and strong such a structure could be. Heidenreichstein Fortress, near the Czechoslovakia border, was begun in the twelfth century. It has very thick walls and towers almost bare of windows so that it reminds one of some of the concrete air-raid shelters erected in Europe during World War II.

In Austria, as in all countries, some castles boast of legends that have grown up around them. At Schattenburg Castle, built in the first half of the twelfth century, there is said to be a ghost who walks at night—the ghost of a knight who is still being punished for some

Hochosterwitz Castle, Austria

Forchtenstein Castle,

Austria

wrong he did hundreds of years ago. At Rabenstein Castle, on high rocks over the Mur River, legend has it that ravens once saved the life of the princess of the castle by eating some poisoned cakes sent her by a lover she had dismissed.

Forchtenstein, in the province of Burgenland, was not built until the sixteenth century and shows how defensive features could be combined with the improved and more comfortable living quarters of those days. It was the only castle in the area not captured during the Turkish invasion of 1683. Among other castles of Austria that bring back stories of the days of knighthood and feudalism are: Clam on the Danube River; Groppenstein; Kufstein in the Tyrol; Landsberg, built in the year 1,000; Laudegg on the Inn River; Raab; and Riegersburg.

Another country that can boast of many castles and their ruins is Switzerland. Perhaps best known is the Castle of Chillon at Montreux because of the poets it has inspired as a result of one dramatic incident in its long history. Started in the ninth century and restored in the thirteenth, Chillon, built on a rock in Lake Geneva, is remembered today chiefly for its dungeon. It was here that the Swiss hero, Francois de Bonivard, was held prisoner from 1530 to 1536 as a result of his revolt against Charles III, Duke of Savoy. Finally, the men of the cities of Berne and Geneva stormed the castle in 1536 and released Bonivard. About 300 years later this inspired the poet Lord

Castle of Chillon, Switzerland

Dungeon of the Castle of Chillon, Switzerland

Byron to write "The Prisoner of Chillon," which includes these descriptive lines:

> "There are seven pillars of Gothic mould,
> In Chillon's dungeons deep and old,
> There are seven columns, mossy and grey,
> Dim with a dull imprison'd ray . . ."

The castle of Beromunster housed the first printing press in Switzerland, in 1470, while the castle of Gruyere, a fine medieval structure in a perfect state of repair, is in the region famous for Gruyere cheese. Near Brugg is the Castle of Hapsburg, built about 1020, and the original birthplace of the House of Hapsburg whose kings and emperors ruled many parts of Europe for hundreds of years. Lenzburg Castle, over 800 years old, is now owned by an American family. The castle of the lords of Tarasp, dating back nearly 1,000 years, was completely renovated and luxuriously furnished as a residence only 50 years ago and now belongs to the former Grand Duke of Hesse. Among other castles still well worth seeing are Hallwyl, Neuchatel, Ortenstein, Sargans, and Spiez.

Castle of the Hapsburgs, Switzerland

Castle of the Counts of Flanders, Belgium

Belgium, another country with a long history, has its share of interesting castles. At Ghent the city grew around a castle started on a small island in the ninth century by the first Count of Flanders, Baldwin Bras-de-Fer (meaning "iron arm"). Rebuilt in 1180 by Philip of Alsace, it had 24 towers and was modeled after the Crusaders' castles in Syria. It now houses a collection of instruments of torture.

71

Franchimont in Liege Province is believed to be the birthplace of Charles Martel (688?-741) of the powerful Carolingian family that ruled much of Western Europe for many years. Charles Martel was the grandfather of the most famous of the Carolingians, the Emperor Charlemagne. Charlemagne's father, by the way, was a king known as Pepin the Short and his mother was called Bertha of the Big Foot. The medieval castle at Franchimont was built in the twelfth century.

A castle first built in 1085 was in the news as recently as 1940. This is Wynendaele, once a favorite residence of the Counts of Flanders. It sheltered the Belgian royal family in 1940 when the Nazis invaded the country and it was here that King Leopold III informed high government officials that he had decided to remain in Belgium and share the fate of the army. Belgium is also famous for other ancient castles such as: Walzin and Spontin in Namur Province; Beersel and Gaasbeek near Brussels; and Bouillon and La Roche in Luxembourg Province.

Beersel Castle,

Belgium

Kronborg Castle, Denmark

Most of the castles now standing in Denmark are fairly new as castles go, but some of them are on the sites of much older fortresses. Best known is Kronborg Castle in the town of Elsinore. A castle was first erected here in the twelfth century at a strategically important spot on the coast. The present buildings, however, were put up between 1574 and 1585. Elsinore is world-famous as the scene of one of Shakespeare's most important plays, "Hamlet." Down under the ramparts of Kronborg Castle is the statue of Holger Danske (Ogier the Dane) who, according to legend, will awake and take up his sword to defend Denmark when the country is in danger.

This account of a few of the castles of Europe is by no means complete, but it does indicate how extensive the building of castles was and how important a part they played in history for many centuries. Castles were not erected for fun or for romantic reasons. Castles were built for practical purposes and they grew naturally out of the conditions of life and the kind of government of the Middle Ages. They changed as time passed, becoming bigger and stronger as men devised ways to make them so, and as other men found more powerful weapons and methods of attacking them.

VI   Defending and Capturing a Castle

W HEN A KING or a noble built a castle in the Middle Ages, he expected that it would be attacked by his enemies, perhaps many times. A castle, in the true sense, was both a home for a feudal lord and a private fortress. As a fortress, it had two purposes: it could be used by the lord and his soldiers and retainers to rule the surrounding countryside; and it was a stronghold in which the lord, his family, and his followers could defend themselves against another lord who came to attack them.

It is not surprising, then, that much time and thought and effort were given to the two problems of defense and offense. How could castles be made stronger so that they would be more difficult to capture? How could those attacking castles devise more powerful weapons that would enable them to overcome the defenders? Whatever one side did, the other tried to think up an answer that would put it back in the lead.

Basically, there were three ways to take a castle: by a surprise attack; by treachery; or by a siege. A siege might be successful in one of two ways. The besiegers could break down the castle's walls so that an assault by their forces would gain access to the castle; or, the siege could simply go on until the defenders surrendered because they were starving or because disease had broken out in the castle.

Surprise attacks were most successful in the early days of castles when walls were not so high, when ditches were not so deep, and when the garrison in the castle was not well disciplined and on the alert.

As castles came to be built of stone, with higher walls, great watch-towers, strongly defended gates, and other devices, it became increasingly difficult to catch the castle by surprise and to burst into its courtyard before the garrison was aware of what was going on. Treachery, on the other hand, might take place any time and in any kind of castle if there were some of the garrison who could be bribed, or who decided they favored the other side of the fight. They might turn on the commander of the castle and those who remained faithful to him, or they might leave the gate unguarded, or allow the enemy to climb up over a certain part of the wall. The always present possibility of treachery is one reason why the lord, or the commander of the garrison, began to have his quarters in a stronger gatehouse, or a keep, where he was cut off from the soldiers and could defend himself against them if necessary.

The art of defending and of capturing a castle is best seen in an account of what is known as siegecraft. This simply means the methods and equipment used by an army to try to capture a strongly defended site, such as a castle. On the defenders' side, a number of things were learned and used that made it more difficult to besiege a castle successfully. First of all, the thicker and higher the stone walls the better—until the fourteenth century when gunpowder began to be used to fire cannons. Two rings of walls around the castle were better than one, and round towers were somewhat stronger than square ones, whose corners gave way more easily when undermined.

The tops of walls and towers were improved to aid in fighting off the enemy. The battlement, an indented parapet at the top of a castle wall, had raised parts called merlons, and indentations, through which the defenders could fire on the attackers, called embrasures or crenelles. When the top of a wall or tower was constructed in this way it was said to be crenelated. As both construction and military ideas advanced, the battlements were built so that they extended out over the top of the wall or tower on the outside. The people of Europe got this idea from the Moslems during the Crusades. The projections that supported these battlements were called corbels. Between the

75

The Battlements of a Castle

corbels were openings known as machicolations. The purpose of these was to enable the defenders to fire almost straight down on any enemy and to drop rocks, molten lead, boiling water, or anything else available on the heads of the attackers.

The siege of a castle began when a strong attacking force of many soldiers with special equipment surrounded a castle with its defenders inside. Usually, this meant that the attacking force outnumbered the soldiers inside the castle. From the point of view of the attacking force, there were three ways for them to capture the castle: they had either to get over, or under, or through the walls. And by around the year 1300, when castle building was at its best but when artillery had not yet appeared, a blockade and siege of a castle was about the only way to capture it.

The defenders, on their part, might even make sorties: they might rush suddenly out of a gate and attack some of the besieging force, perhaps to destroy some of their siege equipment. On the other hand, the defenders were encircled and shut in, even if they made a few sorties, and this could be discouraging and boring, and lead to a loss of morale. Sometimes the besiegers, on their part, had to break down the walls within a certain length of time before the king, or some other ally of the castle's lord, could send a relief force to attack the attackers of the castle.

The first defense of the castle was the moat, the water-filled ditch around it, and this was the first obstacle the besiegers had to overcome. They would try to fill it in with whatever material was handy. The men who had this job would be protected to some extent by their comrades who would fire arrows and larger missiles at the defenders. The people in the castle would try to shoot the men filling in the moat. Until the moat was filled in, the siege force could not try to capture the castle by putting ladders up against the walls (called escalading), nor could they get near enough the walls to use battering rams. An unfilled moat hindered mining, since the water might break through and flood the tunnel being dug underneath it.

Mining was an effective, but long and dangerous, way of breaking down a castle's defenses. Men would start digging, first down and then under the ground toward the castle. A mine could be used in one of two ways. It could create a passageway so that attacking soldiers could rush through it when it was finished and come up inside the castle. More likely though, the object of the mine would be to cause a tower or part of a wall to collapse. As the mine was dug, its sides and roof would be supported by timbers. When it was under the right spot the timbers, and other combustible material placed in the mine, would be set on fire. Then, the besiegers hoped, the fire would cause the timbers to collapse and that in turn would bring down the roof of the mine and the wall above it. This would create a gap, or breach, and the attackers would attempt to rush through it and overwhelm the garrison.

77

Since it was almost impossible to keep secret the fact that a mine was being dug, the defenders could take action early. Naturally, they would fire on the miners and attempt to keep them from their labor. So the besiegers built a penthouse, which was a shelter over the men where they were working. It was built of heavy logs or timber, covered with clay and hides, and with sloping roofs so that missiles would glance off. Sometimes the whole thing, especially the hides, would be soaked with water to prevent fires being set by torches, pitch, or whatever might be hurled down from the walls. The defenders also might start a countermine, heading it toward where they thought the besiegers' mine was coming. If they could break in, they could cause the mine to collapse on top of the miners or they could attack them and drive them out.

Another common way of attempting to take a castle was to use a battering ram. This is a very old method and basically consists simply of driving the end of a beam against a wall or gate until it is broken down. Later, a metal cap was put on the battering ram to strengthen it, and it was suspended by ropes so it could be swung back and forth. Still later it was laid on rollers and impelled by ropes. Toward the end of the Middle Ages, the battering ram had become a very large contraption, mounted on wheels, with a roof over it to protect the men. It might be from 60 to 120 feet long and it took as many as 100 men to operate it. To speed up the attack and to give the defenders no rest, a ram might be operated by two or more shifts of soldiers.

Somewhat like the battering ram was the bore. It was smaller, lighter, and took fewer people to operate. It had an armored but sharper head because it was used to attempt to drill a hole near the base of a wall as a starting point for undermining the foundations by further digging. When attackers used either the ram or the bore, the defenders tried to stop them by catching hold of the end of it with a forked beam or a hook.

Another piece of equipment used in the attack was a tower, or belfry. This was built very high, because its purpose was to provide the attackers with a means of reaching the same height as the defend-

A Ram

ers on top of the walls. It was erected on wheels and rolled up to the wall after the moat was filled in. Like the penthouses protecting the ram, the bore, and the miners, these towers had to be covered with wood, hides, and anything else that would hold off the arrows fired from the castle. The towers sometimes had drawbridges that could be let down on to the top of the castle wall, so that the attackers could rush across and attempt to capture the castle by hand-to-hand combat. Another use of the tower was to keep a rain of missiles on the defenders so that they in turn could not do much to fire on men starting such operations as mining.

Soldiers wore some kind of armor as they attacked or defended a castle. Just what they wore depended on two things. One was the era in which they lived, because armor got more and more complete —and also heavier—as the Middle Ages went on. The other was a matter of who they were: lords and knights wore better and heavier armor; the lower-class foot soldiers, or infantry, had less armor. This was not, however, as important in besieging castles as in battles fought in the open between two armies. A knight in full armor and mounted on his horse was a powerful force in open battle, but he couldn't charge a castle wall. Attackers did need protection, but it had to be such that they could move around on foot as they worked

The Longbow

The Crossbow

their machinery or fired their weapons. The soldiers in the castle were less in need of armor because they had the walls to protect them.

Both sides were armed with hand weapons as well as larger instruments of war. The bow and arrow in the age of the castle was the equivalent of the rifle and revolver today. Attackers and besiegers used the bow and arrow for two purposes. One was to kill or wound as many of the enemy as possible, so that the besiegers would be discouraged by their losses and go away; or so that the defenders would become so few they would have to surrender. The other purpose was more defensive. If the besiegers were about to try to fill in the moat, for example, the bowmen would keep up a steady fire on the defenders on the walls and towers so that they, in turn, would be prevented from firing their arrows down upon the men filling in the moat.

There were two kinds of bows. One was the crossbow, which was a bow set on a stock so that the bow was parallel with the ground rather than standing up from it. It was stronger than an ordinary bow and it could fire stone and metal as well as arrows, but it was slow and hard to work. The other was the longbow, which came into

81

its own around the end of the thirteenth century. The skill of the English longbowmen became such that they were the most terrifying and powerful soldiers of Europe for many years. The longbow, standing about the same height as a man, had a range of up to 250 yards, and an expert bowman could fire six to eight arrows a minute. Only a few of these famous weapons survive today. One was dug up at Berkhampstead Castle and may date from the siege of 1217 in which 1,000 Sussex bowmen are said to have taken part.

The most impressive weapons used in the siege of a castle were the implements of war that were in those days the equivalent of the artillery—the cannons and rockets—of today. The history of big siege weapons goes back to the fifth century B.C. Alexander the Great developed enormous slings and catapults, and the Romans were most successful and efficient in using them against their enemies. As in castle building, the people of Europe who succeeded the Romans did not for some time improve upon these weapons. They were used and gradually improved for well over 300 years, from the start of castle building until they were replaced by artillery. Chief among these siege weapons, and good examples of the main types, were the balista, the catapult, and the trebuchet.

The balista was an enormous crossbow, mounted on a stand.

A Balista

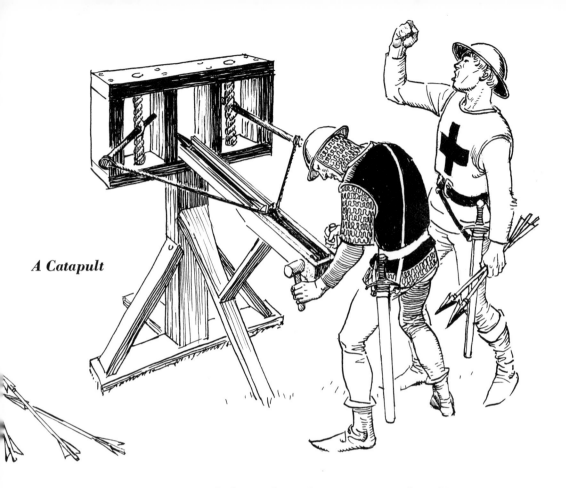

A Catapult

Powerful models could fire a bolt weighing five or six pounds a distance of 500 yards. The balista could fire iron darts, or heavy arrows, or stones. Where the catapult and the trebuchet threw their shots in a high arc so that they came down on the heads of the enemy, the balista fired its arrow faster and on more of a straight line. Thus it was more like a modern field-artillery piece, while the other two weapons were the equivalent of today's howitzers. The balista was not powerful enough to do much damage to castle walls but could be a strong weapon against enemy soldiers and their equipment.

The catapult was like a giant slingshot, which sometimes was mounted on wheels and other times was built at the spot where it was needed. It had a revolving arm with a skein of sinew which was twisted to the limit. The arm was then held down and the shot placed either in a cup-shaped depression at the end of the arm or in a sling fastened to the end. When the arm was suddenly released, the twisted sinews pulled the arm up and forward and the shot was discharged. Stones were used and a 50 pound one could be hurled 500 yards with considerable accuracy. The Arabs said that at the siege of Acre in 1191 the Crusaders used 300 catapults and balistae.

The trebuchet was simpler but larger than the catapult and even-

A Trebuchet

tually replaced it. It had a large, revolving arm. At the end of the long part of the arm was the place for the shot; at the short end was a heavy counterweight. The long part of the arm was held down and when it was suddenly released the force of gravity pulled it up fast and its missile was discharged. Thus it was somewhat like a gigantic see-saw. It could hurl a 200 or 300 pound projectile about 600 yards, and some of the largest trebuchets had arms 50 feet long and counterweights of ten tons. Usually it hurled large stones, but on occasion it is reported to have thrown dead horses into a castle or town in the hope of causing disease. A spy of the defending forces might be caught, killed, and returned to the castle by firing him over the walls in the trebuchet.

Edward I of England designed a colossal trebuchet for the siege of Stirling Castle in Scotland and put 50 carpenters and five foremen to work on it. However, the castle surrendered before the trebuchet was ready. At another siege of Acre, this one in 1291, the Crusaders used a trebuchet that required 100 carts to haul all its parts and pieces. One of the last occasions on which a trebuchet was used— and this was long after they had gone out of general use—was in 1480 at the siege of Rhodes. The Turks, attacking the town, had cannons, but not very good ones. The defenders built a trebuchet and it did more damage to the attackers than they could do with their newer-style weapon. The final appearance of the trebuchet may have been at the siege of Mexico City by Cortez in 1521. When the Spaniards ran out of ammunition for their guns, one of the soldiers thought he could design a trebuchet that would take the place of the artillery. Unfortunately for him, there was something wrong with his design. When it was fired the missile went up in the air but came back down on top of the machine instead of the city.

While the weapons just described were necessary in besieging a castle, they could also be used by the defenders to keep the attackers away from the castle walls and to destroy the machines and weapons they were using. These weapons, and almost any other, could be used by either side to throw an incendiary, that being simply any

missile that was burning. Rags or other material were soaked in pitch and fired into a castle by tying the burning rags around an arrow or other projectile.

The builders of castles developed various little tricks to make it more difficult for the enemy. Entrance ways, leading up to the main gate, might be quite long, with several right-angle turns in them. This meant that as any attacker turned a corner, the defenders could be waiting to fire on him down the passage. Even the building of stair-cases had its tricks. The spiral stairs in castle towers were constructed so that anyone going down them was always turning to the left. This kept the person's right arm, or sword arm, free and clear, while any-one attempting to fight his way up the stairs would have his sword arm cramped against the inside wall of the staircase.

With huge and powerful walls, together with tricks and strata-gems, the builders and defenders of castles had the upper hand most of the time for about 400 years. It became almost impossible to cap-ture a castle except by starving the inhabitants, and the best weapons devised could do little to break down the defenses of a well-com-manded castle. Then all of this ended about the middle of the four-teenth century when the introduction of gunpowder into Europe caused a radical change in all forms of warfare.

The first gun may have been that devised by Berthold Schwarz, a German monk, in 1313. Certainly guns were used at the battle of Crecy in 1346. These early artillery pieces were not very efficient or powerful. No one yet knew how to make good gun barrels, and stones were still used as the missile fired by the gun. However, within 100 years the making and using of guns had been improved to such an extent that castles were almost worse than useless. Before, the higher the wall the more difficult it was to capture the castle; now, the higher the wall the better the target it made. Cannon became much more powerful than any of the old weapons such as the trebuchet. Guns could blow the defenders off the battlements and punch big holes in walls and gates.

In 1415 King Henry V of England besieged Harfleur in Normandy and with the aid of artillery guns captured it in a little more than a month, thus establishing the supremacy of the new artillery over medieval fortifications. King Henry had 75 artillerymen, the first organized British artillery. His guns even had names, such as "Lon-don," "Messenger," and "King's Daughter." By 1450 King Charles VII of France had so powerful a siege train of guns that he captured all the castles in Normandy held by the English in one year. However, artillery had become so expensive and required such skilled men to operate it that only a king could afford to have it in his army.

The castle, while as interesting and romantic as ever, was losing its important place in the world, partly because of these new artillery weapons, but also for other reasons.

VII   The End of the Age of Castles

FOR ABOUT 400 years—from the eleventh into the fifteenth century—
castles played an important part in the life of the people of Europe,
from kings to peasants. Then, for several reasons, the day of the
castle was over.

One reason was the introduction of weapons using gunpowder,
but other reasons could be found in events which had been going on
slowly almost from the time castles were first built. For many years
in most of the countries of Europe, the king's central government
had been becoming more powerful and ruling the land more directly,
instead of through the feudal nobles in their castles. Also, the increase
in population, the growth of towns, and the expansion of commerce
over larger areas brought into importance a new class of business
people who did not want to be bothered by a great number of petty
nobles scattered all over the country.

As a factor in warfare, the castle was affected in two ways by
these changes. In the first place, the great castle with its high walls
and towers was no longer almost impossible to capture. Instead,
artillery could blast the walls apart. In the second place, with the system of feudalism dying out, and with the national states such as England, France, and Spain growing powerful, there was no need for a
great number of castles scattered all over the country. Instead, fortifications were needed on coast lines, at the mouths of rivers, and at
boundaries between countries. War now was between nations rather
than between individual feudal nobles.

As a result, some castles were rebuilt to make them useful under the new conditions. In other places, new forts were built. These were somewhat like the old castles, but differed both in the way they were constructed and in the fact that they were purely military posts of a strong national government instead of combination homes and fortresses of nobles. Walls were built lower, and it was found that great mounds of earth were better protection against artillery fire than were high stone walls. The walls could be blown apart by guns, and the pieces flew all over the place like hundreds of small bullets. An earth wall, on the other hand, let artillery missiles penetrate a short way, but then tended to absorb and smother the blast.

There are a number of interesting examples in England of castles that were changed to meet new conditions, or that were built too late to be true castles even though they bear that name. Bodiam Castle

Bodiam Castle, England

Dartmouth Castle, England

in Sussex was built in 1386 and looks much like the great Edwardian castles of a century earlier. Actually, it differs in several ways. It was built for coastal defense against a possible French invasion. It is much more comfortable inside than earlier castles. And Bodiam has openings in its walls that were the new style for artillery guns. Instead of the usual arrow-slit, these openings are circular at the bottom, so that they look like a keyhole and allow cannon to be fired from inside the castle. In other respects, Bodiam is like its powerful predecessors. It was approached by a causeway over a large moat, and there were no less than three portcullises on the way.

Dartmouth, a port in Devonshire from which Richard the Lion-Hearted set out on his Crusade to the Holy Land in 1190, is the site of an interesting structure that deserves the name castle in some

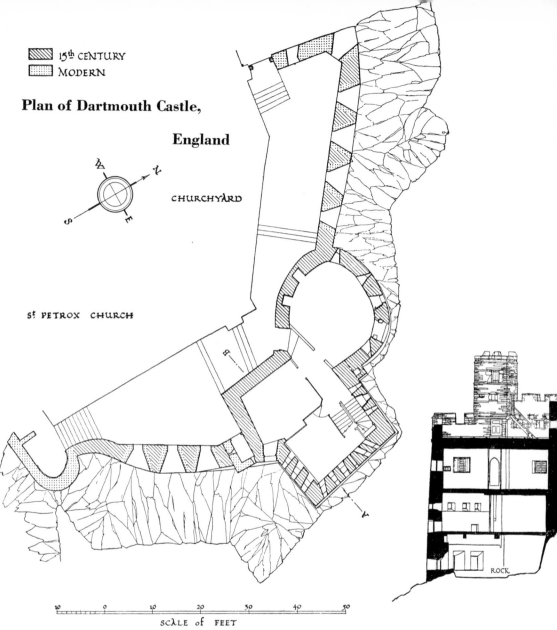

15th CENTURY
MODERN

Plan of Dartmouth Castle,

England

CHURCHYARD

S⁺ PETROX CHURCH

SCALE of FEET

SECTION ON A-B

respects. Although there are some remains of a medieval castle near-by, the present fort dates from 1481. It was not built then by a feudal lord but rather by King Edward IV and the officials of the town of Dartmouth. From the beginning Dartmouth Castle was a fortress

92

to defend the coast and the port from foreign invaders, and so its strong walls and towers face the sea without going all the way around to make the older and true style of castle. The gun ports (the openings through which those in the castle could fire the new artillery) were the most advanced in style in all of England at the time they were built. They were, as a matter of fact, the first to show a real change from the adaptations of the arrow-slit kind of opening in castle walls.

Pendennis Castle on the Cornwall coast is on the site of a prehistoric fortification, but the castle was not built until about 1545 by King Henry VIII when there was again danger that the French would invade England. In plan, King Henry's castle looks like an older, round keep, surrounded by a curtain wall. But there is a very important difference. The gun ports are "splayed," that is, they are wider on the outside than on the inside so that the guns could be swung back and forth to cover a wider area. Then, in 1598 when there were rumors of a second Spanish Armada attacking England,

Pendennis Castle, England

Plan of Pendennis Castle, England

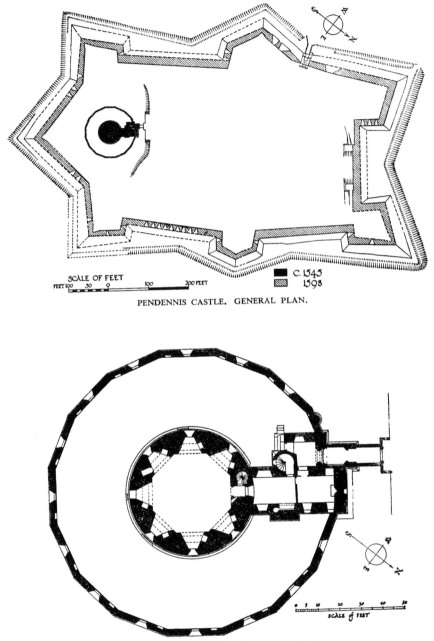

PENDENNIS CASTLE. GENERAL PLAN.

SCALE OF FEET

C. 1545
1598

PLAN OF THE CASTLE OF HENRY VIII.

King Henry's daughter, Queen Elizabeth I, had a modern style, low, thick wall with openings for cannon built in a rectangle on the high ground around the older castle. The guns used in this era at Pendennis Castle were iron or brass, mounted on wooden carriages. They fired stone or cast-iron balls. There were accommodations in the castle for the soldiers of the garrison who were armed with muskets and calivers (heavy guns that had to be fired from a rest). Normally there were from 100 to 400 soldiers, reinforced in times of danger by men from the neighboring countryside. In World War I this castle was part of the coast defenses of England and at the start of World War II the British Army once again took it over.

Finally, there is Dover Castle in Kent. An important port for almost 2,000 years, Dover can still show on the site of its castle what is left of a lighthouse the Romans built before A.D. 100. The first castle here, an oval enclosure surrounded by a ditch and an earth bank, was constructed by King Harold just a few years before he was defeated by William the Conqueror at Hastings in 1066. King Henry II in the twelfth century used masonry to improve the castle. Dover became one of the strongest castles in England and, although improved from time to time, remained essentially the same for over 500 years. Then came the great transformation of the late eighteenth century when the threat of an invasion by Napoleon's French forces caused the castle to be adapted to the needs of the times. Here is a good example of the return to earthworks as a better defense than masonry walls. A bank of earth was piled against the outer curtain of the castle all the way around. The towers were filled up solid and levelled as platforms on which to put cannon. A century and a half later, in World War II, the castle again contained important military installations. Although Dover was under continual bombardment from the air and from the French coast, it escaped any serious damage.

While castles were changing in these various ways, other things were going on in the world that affected them and the people who built and owned them. The feudal manor had been based on agriculture. The lord of the manor had his castle, his vassals, and his

95

Dover Castle, England

serfs. The lord and his fighting men ruled and defended the manor, or attacked the enemy; the serfs grew the food, made the cloth, and produced practically all the things everyone needed to live. Compared with the system of living we know today, almost no money was needed.

But all during the Middle Ages the population was growing, trade was increasing, and more people were dependent upon the towns and upon business rather than upon the feudal nobles and their manors. There was an increase of communication as more people traveled to more places. Even the Crusades helped end the feudal system by spreading knowledge of the world and causing people to move around more. The people of the towns wanted stable government over a large area. They wanted to be able to transport and sell their goods without danger of robbery or of excess and unexpected taxes forced on them by some baron in a castle built at a strategic crossroads. So the new and growing class of business people sided with the king and the strong central government that could give them what they needed to do business. At the same time, the king and his officials found that co-operating with the new merchant class had its advantages. They could collect taxes in money, and with that money they could hire soldiers, build warships, and construct castles. Then they were no longer dependent on the personal services of feudal knights, and with their superior power in soldiers and guns they could rule a whole nation without the once powerful lords.

Thus it was that feudalism gradually died out. It was gone by the end of the sixteenth century in England and France. In some other countries it lingered longer. The year 1492, in which Columbus discovered America, is often used as a convenient date for the end of the Middle Ages. It was about this same time that printing was invented in Europe and that there was a Renaissance, or rebirth, of the fine arts. Many castles and many noble families remained, but with each passing year both the feudal system and its most formidable symbol, the castle, became of less and less importance in the actual running of the world.

What happened to the castles and the people who built and owned them? As already indicated, many of the castles still exist. Some became fortresses used for the military purposes of the king and his central government. Some were deliberately destroyed by the king to further reduce the power of the nobles. This was known as "slighting" and consisted of undermining a wall or tower enough so that the castle could not be defended. It would have been too expensive and taken too long to tear down to the ground a whole castle.

Kings and nobles and rich people went on building magnificent homes and many of them continued to look more or less like castles, but they could not be defended the way the old-time castles could. The kings of the sixteenth to the eighteenth centuries built palaces which were enormous homes, much more comfortable and luxurious than the medieval castles. The word palace, incidentally, comes from Palatine Hill, one of the seven hills on which Rome was built. The Emperor Augustus constructed there what became the palace of the Caesars. Buckingham Palace in London, erected in 1703 and purchased by King George III in 1761, is an excellent example of the new kind of royal home.

Handsome country houses and elegant city mansions were built by, and became the homes of, men and women who in previous centuries would have lived in castles. The word chateau is often applied to the fine country homes, especially those in France. Castles stood on sites which dominated the area, but the chateaux, or country homes, were more likely to be set back in their own parks surrounded by gardens and trees. Beauty and comfort became as important as power and protection had once been.

It is a tribute to the skill of their construction and the strength of the materials that so many hundreds of castles still stand today. Some of them are in ruins, but many of them are being lived in right now. In countries boasting old castles, many are kept in good repair and are open to visitors. Often guides are provided to explain the history of the castle and the contents—interesting and valuable collections of furniture, art, and other things. In Scotland, for example, the

Duke of Argyll, who is head of the Clan Campbell among other honors, has opened his ancestral home, Inverary Castle, to visitors for a fee of about 35 cents. In Germany and Austria, many of the famous and imposing castles have been turned into hotels and a visitor can "live like a nobleman." Anyone taking a trip to any of the countries boasting famous old castles will want to visit some of them. This can easily be arranged, and the tourist-information bureaus of the various countries are most co-operative in supplying information and attractive descriptive material.

Whether castles are in ruins, or are now being used as hotels for tourists, they still remind us of an age that seems more romantic than ours. The age of castles lacked many conveniences we know today and was full of many dangers. Yet castles represent an important and exciting stage in the development of our civilization. It is thus fitting, and not surprising, that tribute is still paid to castles in poetry and in stories.

Even postage stamps honor castles. In 1956 Great Britain issued a series of four handsome stamps of high value, ranging up to one pound, each showing Queen Elizabeth II and a castle from one of the four parts of her realm: Windsor Castle (England); Edinburgh Castle (Scotland); Caernarvon Castle (Wales); and Carrickfergus Castle (Northern Ireland).

This is merely one of the latest examples of the continuing interest in castles. They have long been used by storytellers and poets as symbols—gay, somber, impressive, magnificent—of things we all dream of. Without really thinking where the inspiration first came from, we all still use such expressions as "castles in the air," and "castles in Spain," and "a man's house is his castle." It will be a long time, if ever, before people forget all about castles.

INDEX